ACCENT ON Christmas & Holiday ENSEMBLES

Duets and trios for flexible instrumentation correlated with ACCENT ON ACHIEVEMENT, Book 1

B♭

John O'Reilly and Mark Williams

Dear Band Student:

Congratulations on becoming a member of the **band!** Another fun way to make music is to play in an **ensemble.** When you perform duets and trios with your friends, you become even more skilled as a musician. This book features Christmas and holiday ensembles correlated with specific pages in *Accent on Achievement*, Book 1, and is playable by students working in any first-year band method. You can play these ensembles with like instruments or with any combination of mixed instruments. Have fun making music together as you perform with *Accent on Christmas and Holiday Ensembles!*

John O'Reilly   Mark Williams

TABLE OF CONTENTS

JINGLE BELLS

James Pierpont
(1822–1893)

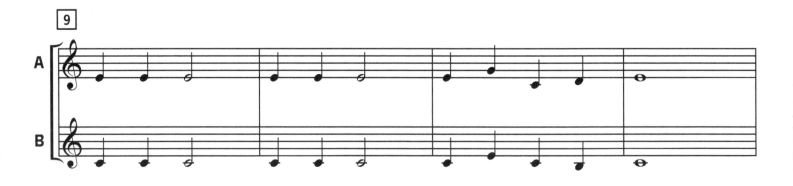

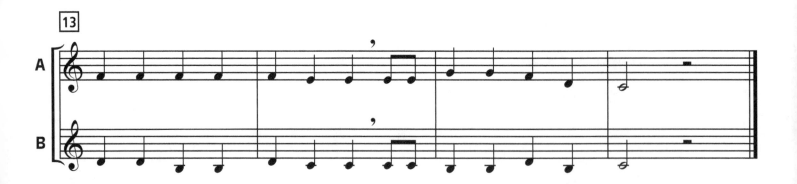

JOLLY OLD ST. NICHOLAS

Traditional

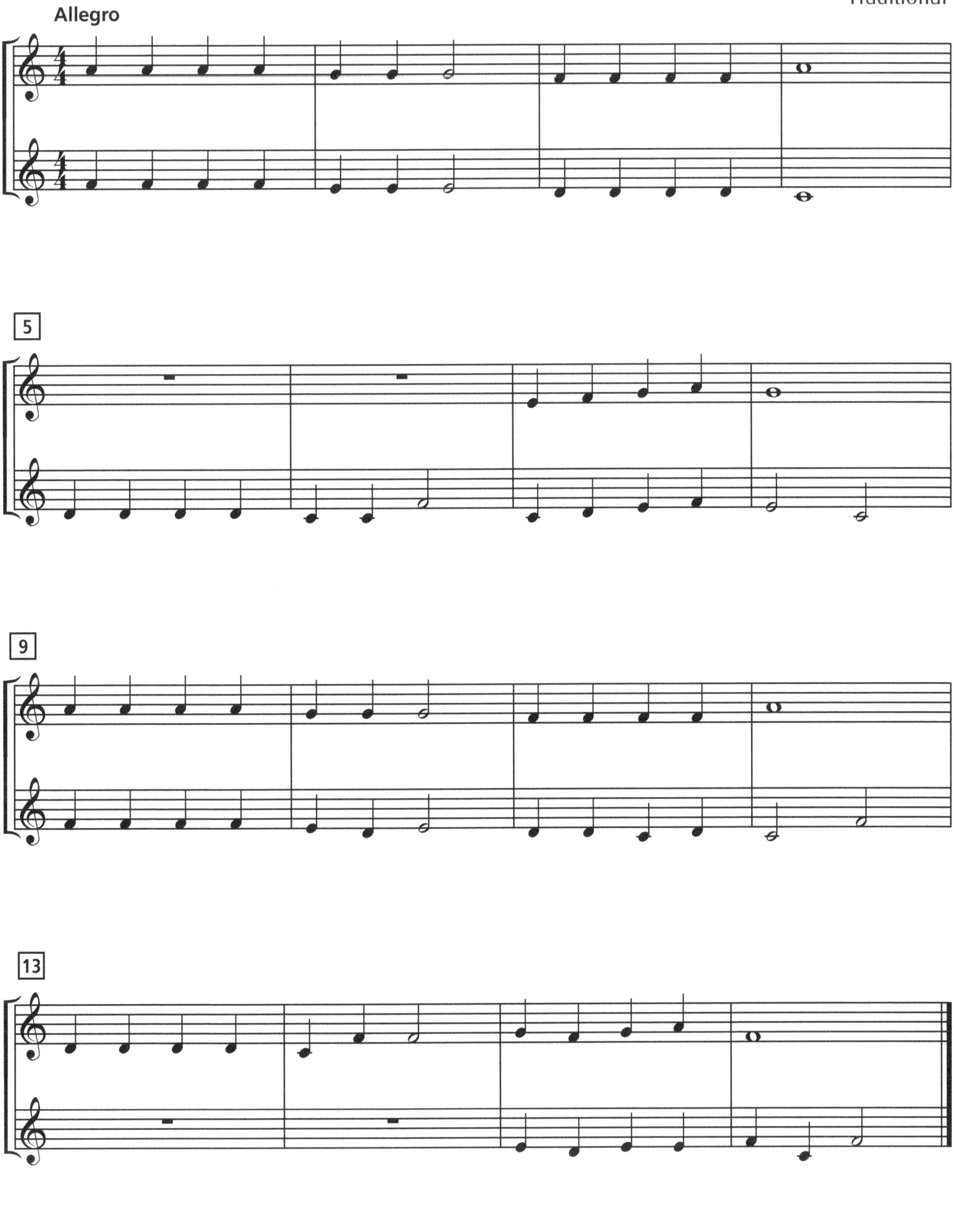

Up on the Housetop

Benjamin Hanby
(1833–1867)

GOOD KING WENCESLAS

Traditional English Carol
(based on a Swedish Folk Song)

Moderato

African Noel

Liberian Folk Song

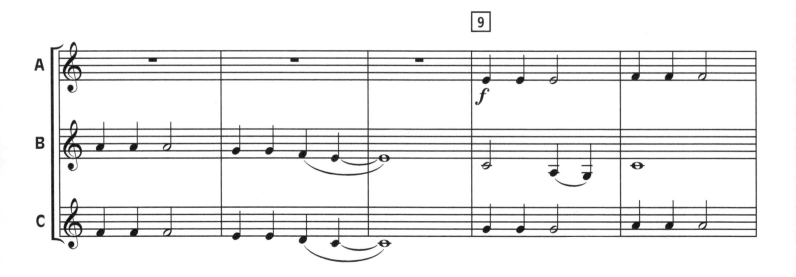

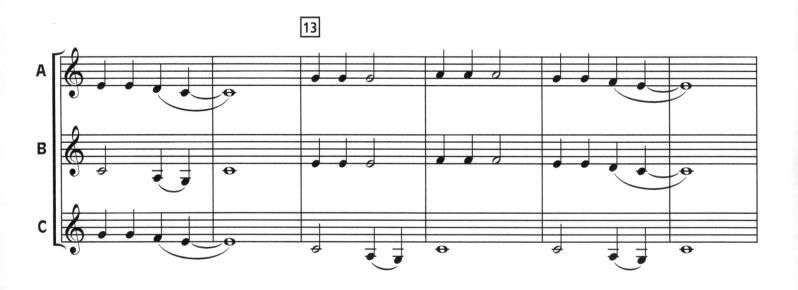

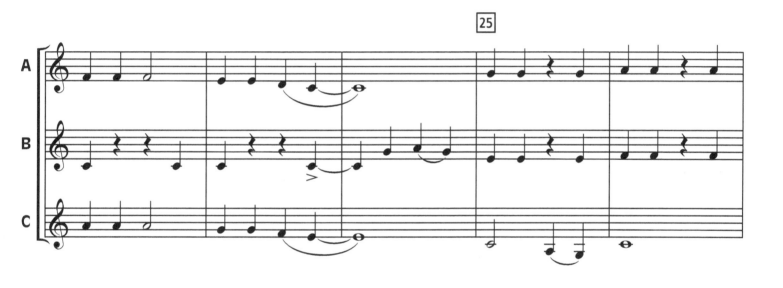

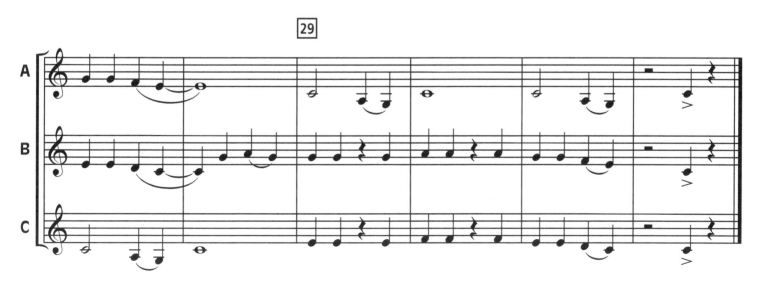

HANUKKAH, HANUKKAH

Traditional

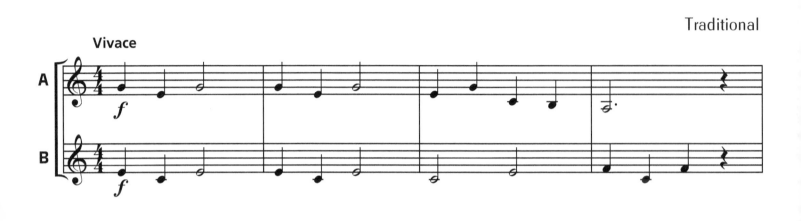

BRING A TORCH, JEANETTE, ISABELLA

French Carol

Moderato

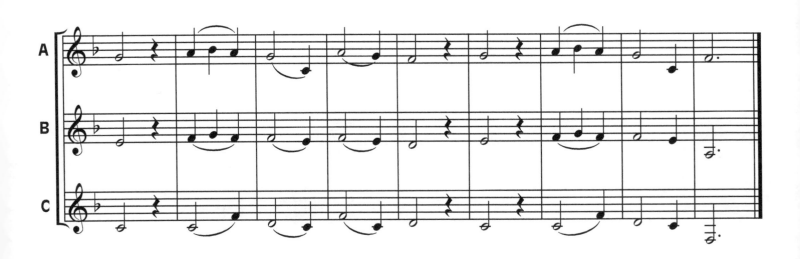

DREYDL SONG

Traditional Hanukkah Song

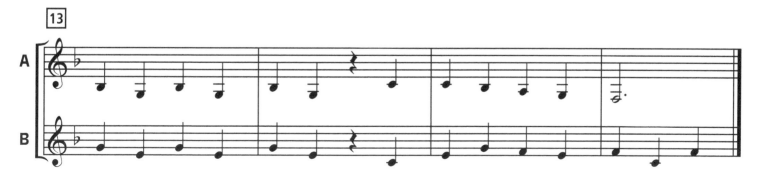

WE WISH YOU A MERRY CHRISTMAS

English Folk Song

O Come, O Come Emmanuel

13th-Century Plainsong

Andante

DECK THE HALLS

Traditional Welsh Carol

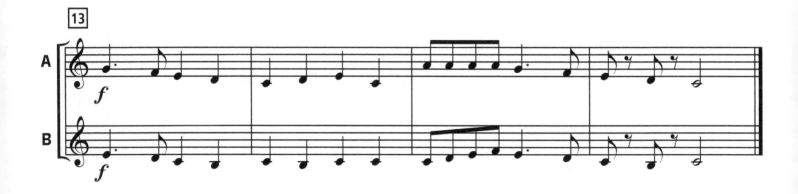

JOY TO THE WORLD

George F. Handel
(1685–1759)

AWAY IN A MANGER

James Murray
(1841–1905)

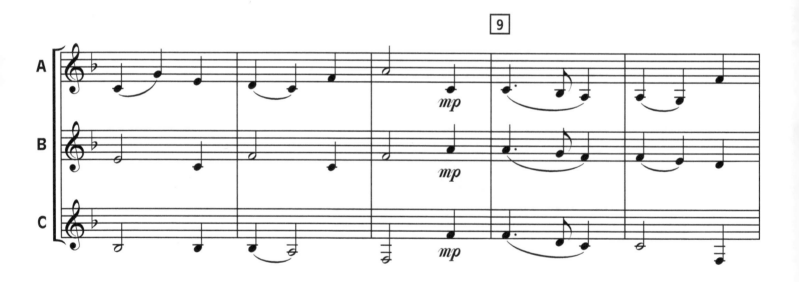

WE THREE KINGS

John Hopkins
(1820–1891)

THE FIRST NOEL

French-English Carol

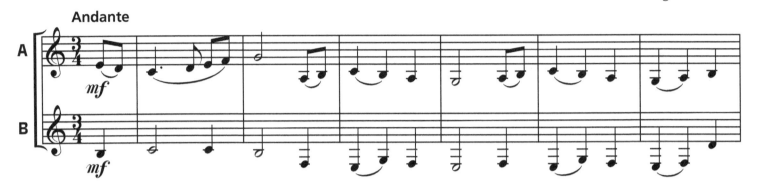

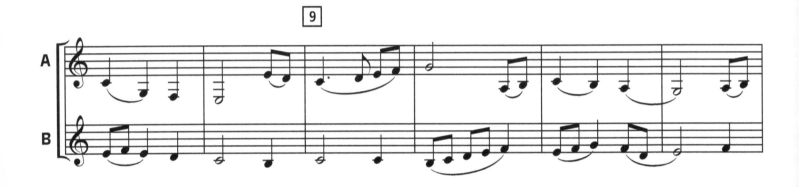

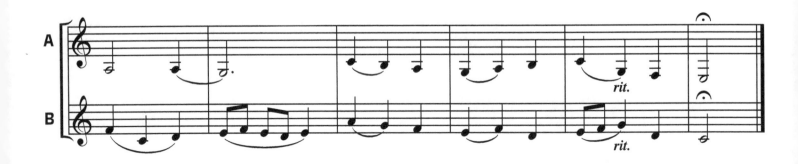

ANGELS FROM THE REALMS OF GLORY

Henry Smart
(1813–1879)

HARK! THE HERALD ANGELS SING

Felix Mendelssohn
(1809–1847)

ANGELS WE HAVE HEARD ON HIGH

French-English Carol

HANUKKAH, O HANUKKAH

Traditional

DING, DONG MERRILY ON HIGH

Thoinot Arbeau
(1520–1595)

Auld Lang Syne

Traditional Scottish Air

Andante

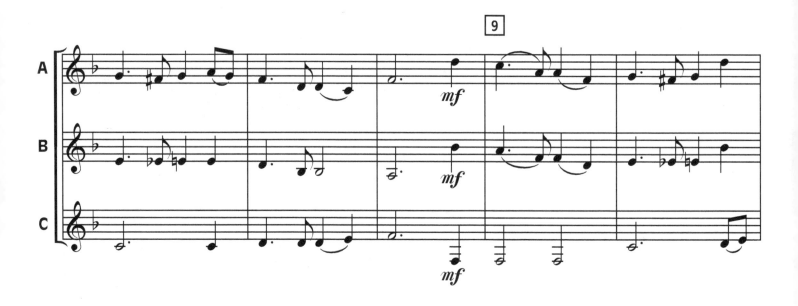